WONDERFUL WORLD OF ENGLISH

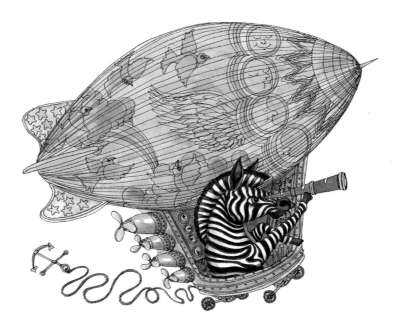

WAY UP HIGH

World Book International
© 1994 World Book, Inc.

World Book, Inc.
a Scott Fetzer company
Chicago   London   Tunbridge Wells   Sydney

Why Is the Sky Blue?

I don't suppose you happen to know
Why the sky is blue? It's because the snow
Takes out the white. That leaves it clean
For the trees and grass to take out the green.
Then pears and bananas start to mellow
And bit by bit they take out the yellow.
The sunsets, of course, take out the red
And pour it into the ocean bed
Or behind the mountains in the west.
You take all that out and the rest
Couldn't be anything else but blue.
—Look for yourself. You can see it's true.

—WHY THE SKY IS BLUE
John Ciardi

This is a fun way to explain why the sky is blue, but of course it isn't true. The sky really gets its colour from the sunlight passing through the air.

Sunlight contains all the colours of the rainbow. As sunlight travels through the air, it bumps into tiny **particles** (pieces) of gas and dust. These particles **scatter** the colours in the sunlight, sending them off in many directions. On a clear day, when the sun is high in the sky, blue is scattered the most of all. So the sky looks blue.

The sky doesn't always look blue, though. At sunrise and sunset, the sun is low in the sky. Its light passes through particles of smoke and dust close to the ground. These particles scatter all the colours except red and orange. So the sun looks like an orange-red ball. And the sky looks red or pink. That's how we get a beautiful sunrise to help start our day and a colourful sunset to wish us good night.

THE FIRST FLYING MACHINE

The first "flying machine" went up into the air on June 4, 1783, in the little town of Vidalon les Annonay, France. The "flying machine" was a big bag made of cloth and paper by two brothers, Étienne and Joseph Montgolfier. The brothers got the bag off the ground by filling it with hot air from a smoky fire. To most people's surprise, the bag floated up about 1,800 metres into the sky! The bag of air looked like a big ball, so people called it a *ballon* (balloon), which means something like "big ball" in French.

Next, the Montgolfier brothers wanted to make a balloon that could carry a person into the sky. However, the king of France said no. He thought it was too dangerous. So the Montgolfier

brothers asked if they could send some animals up in a balloon. The king said yes. On September 19, 1783, the brothers sent up a balloon from the courtyard of the king's palace. A duck, a cockerel, and a sheep rode in a large basket at the bottom of the balloon.

A big crowd of people watched the balloon rise into the air. It went up to about 500 metres before it started to come down. The balloon landed in some trees near the palace. The basket broke open, but all three animals escaped in good condition.

The animals' flight proved that a person could safely go up in a balloon, so the Montgolfier brothers made a new balloon that could carry two people. It was the

biggest balloon they had ever made. A platform hung around the bottom or "neck" of the balloon. The two people could stand on this platform. Inside the neck was an iron pot to hold a fire. Hot air from this fire would keep the balloon flying.

A young French scientist named Jean François Pilâtre de Rozier and his friend François d'Arlandes asked to go up in the balloon. The king said yes. On November 21, 1783, a crowd gathered in a little park outside Paris to watch the two men go up in the balloon. The men stepped onto the platform, and the big balloon slowly filled with hot air. Then something terrible happened! A strong wind pushed the half-filled balloon over and dragged it along the ground. The two men were not hurt, but the balloon was torn.

The Montgolfier brothers did not give up. They soon found someone to sew up the balloon, and tried again to send it up. This time there was no problem. At 1:54 in the afternoon, the balloon rose into the air with the two men on the platform.

A gentle wind pushed the balloon over the rooftops of Paris. Pilâtre de Rozier and d'Arlandes looked down in amazement. As far as we know, they were the first people to see the Earth from high in the sky.

Soon, however, the two men had work to do. The fire in the iron pot was burning tiny holes in the sides of the balloon. To prevent the balloon from burning up, the men let the air in the balloon start to cool. The balloon slowly sank back toward the ground and landed in Paris. Jean François Pilâtre de Rozier and François d'Arlandes were the first two men to fly! They had stayed in the air for almost 25 minutes in the first "flying machine"—a hot-air balloon.

Poems of the Night

The Star

Twinkle, twinkle, little star,
How I wonder what you are,
Up above the world so high,
Like a diamond in the sky.

When the blazing sun is set,
And the grass with dew is wet,
Then you show your little light,
Twinkle, twinkle, all the night.

—Jane Taylor

Moon-Come-Out

Moon-Come-Out
And Sun-Go-In,
Here's a soft blanket
To cuddle your chin.

Moon-Go-In
And Sun-Come-Out,
Throw off the blanket
And bustle about.

—Eleanor Farjeon

8

Star Light, Star Bright

Star light, star bright,
First star I see tonight:
I wish I may, I wish I might
Have the wish I wish tonight.

Working in Space

Someday, you may have a job in space. You may live and work in a **space station** hundreds of kilometres above the Earth.

Space stations probably will be made out of huge metal cylinders and giant flat pieces of metal and plastic. The cylinders will be "buildings" in which people will live and work. The flat pieces will be **solar panels** and **radiator panels**. Solar panels will collect sunlight and turn it into electricity for lighting and heating the station. Radiator panels will collect heat from the cylinders and send it out into space. They will keep the "buildings" from getting too hot.

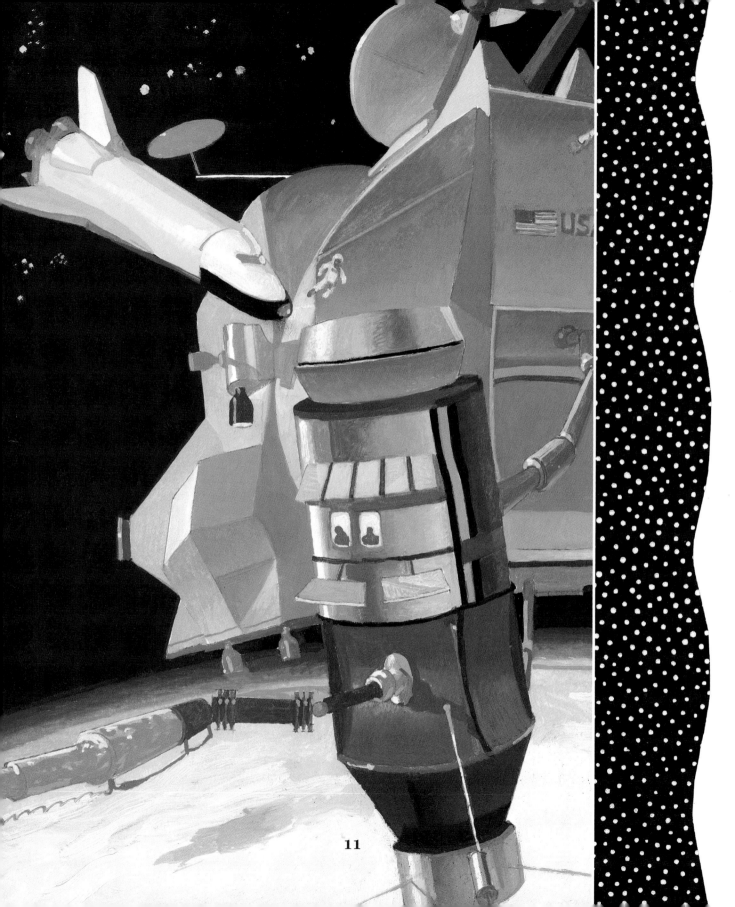

11

Space stations will probably be built in space.

Space shuttles will carry walls, panels, machines, and other equipment out into space. Astronauts will put everything together.

Living in a space station will probably be like living in a submarine. There won't be much room to move around. Machines will provide heat, light, and air conditioning for the cylinder "buildings," so people won't have to wear space suits inside the station.

People working at space stations will do scientific work and experiments. Some space stations might be used as factories to make things people need on Earth.

Space station workers will probably spend about six months at a time out in space, working at their jobs. For a holiday, they will come back down to Earth!

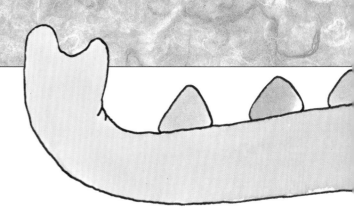

The Creatures of Zorp

Far off in space, four kinds of creatures live on the planet Zorp. Each creature has a different number of legs.

- ☛ Wigglers have four more legs than Gliders.
- ☛ Hoppers have two more legs than Wigglers.
- ☛ Stompers have two fewer legs than Wigglers.
- ☛ Gliders have two legs.

How many legs does each kind of Zorpian creature have?

Find the answer at the back of the book.

Is That Bird a Dinosaur?

At this very minute, there may be a dinosaur in your garden. You don't believe it? Well, it may be true if a bird is flying around. Some scientists believe that birds are a kind of dinosaur!

About 125 years ago, scientists found a stone imprint of a bird they named **archaeopteryx,** which means "ancient wing." We now know archaeopteryx lived about 140 million years ago, during the time of the dinosaurs.

The imprint shows that archaeopteryx looked just like a small dinosaur. It had a long tail; tiny, clawed "hands"; and long jaws filled with sharp teeth. But its body was covered with feathers! It had long feathers on its tail and long feathers on its arms. These feathers show that the "arms" were really wings. Because of the feathers, scientists believe that archaeopteryx was a bird. Perhaps it was even the first kind of bird.

Since archaeopteryx looked so much like a dinosaur, some scientists think its ancestors— and the ancestors of all birds— were dinosaurs. Of course, scientists don't all agree about this. But someday, someone may prove that birds are descendants of the dinosaurs—and really are a kind of dinosaur. If this happens, people may put dinosaur feeders instead of bird feeders in their gardens!

Why the Sun and the Moon Live in the Sky

A folk tale from Africa

Long ago, the Sun and the Water lived together on Earth. They were great friends. Every day they danced and played together on the beach.

The Sun and his wife, the Moon, lived together in a warm, cheery house. The house was painted yellow, pink, and gold. Light danced all around it.

The Water's house was much larger than the Sun's. It was painted blue, green, and violet. A gentle wind blew all around the house, and it was very peaceful.

The Sun often went to the Water's house, but the Water never visited the Sun. One day the Sun asked the Water why he never visited. The Water said, "I would like to visit you, but your house is not big enough for me and all my family. If you build a very large new house, my family and I will be happy to visit you."

The Sun thought this was a wonderful idea. He and the Moon immediately began to build a new house. After a week, the house was finished. It was so big that it stretched as far as the

eye could see. The next day, the Sun and the Moon invited the Water to come for a party.

"May I come in?" the Water asked when he arrived.

"Of course, dear friend," answered the Sun and the Moon.

So the Water and all the members of his family began to come in the doors. Tiny fish, horseshoe crabs, snails, and huge whales poured into the Sun's house.

Soon, the water was knee-deep. "Shall we keep coming in?" the Water asked the Sun. "Of course!" the Sun answered. "The party is just beginning!" So more water entered the house. Now it poured through the

windows as well as the doors.

Soon, the water was high enough to cover a person's head. Again the Water asked the Sun if he and his family could keep coming in. "Of course!" the Sun said again.

Finally, there was so much water in the house that the Sun and the Moon had to sit on the roof. "Should we keep coming in?" the Water asked. The Sun and the Moon were having too much fun to say no. More water and more sea creatures poured into the house, until finally it was completely full. The Sun and the Moon had to go up in the sky, and that is where they have lived ever since.

The Flight to Los Angeles

Can you solve this puzzle?

Two women and a man are passengers on an aeroplane flying from Chicago to Los Angeles. They have the same last names as the pilot, the copilot, and the flight engineer on the plane. Their names are Lee, Brooks, and Navarro.

Read these clues and try to figure out the last names of the pilot, the copilot, and the flight engineer.

Clues

1. Ms. Lee is flying back to her home in Los Angeles.

2. The crew member named Brooks is married to the flight engineer's sister.

3. The passenger with the same last name as the pilot is going on a business trip.

4. The man with the same last name as the copilot lives in Chicago.

5. The passenger whose last name is Brooks is retired.

What is the pilot's last name? What is the copilot's last name? What is the flight engineer's last name?

Find the answers at the back of the book.

The Tale of the Kite

Once, there was a Chinese general who wanted to capture a walled city. The general told his soldiers to dig a tunnel up to and under the wall, and then crawl into the city.

But how long should the tunnel be? To find out, the clever general sent up a kite. When the kite floated over the city, he marked the string.

The length of the string told him how long the tunnel should be. The plan worked, and the city was captured.

This story happened more than two thousand years ago. Kites have been used for many other things since then.

23

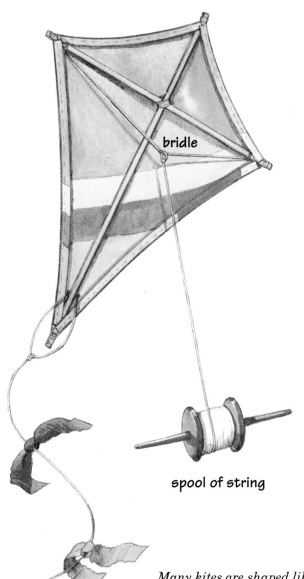

bridle

spool of string

tail

In 1752, a famous American scientist named Ben Franklin tied a metal key to a kite and flew it during a thunderstorm. He wanted to prove that lightning is electricity. When lightning made the key spark, Franklin knew that he was right.

Other people have used kites to test weather conditions and to try out ideas for making aeroplanes. Mostly, though, people fly kites just for fun. In some countries, people even fly kites to celebrate special holidays.

Many kites are shaped like diamonds. They are made of cloth or paper attached to a T-shaped wooden frame. String is tied to the sides of the kite to make a V-shaped **bridle***. The bridle is tied to a long spool of string. The* **tail** *of the kite is tied to the bottom of the frame. It helps to keep the kite pointed toward the sky.*

24

Make Your Own Little Kite

You will need

✪ a piece of construction paper ✪ scissors ✪ a paper punch ✪ paper reinforcements ✪ a spool of thin string or nylon line ✪ one large paper handkerchief ✪ a small paper clip ✪ a ruler ✪ a pencil ✪ markers or crayons (optional)

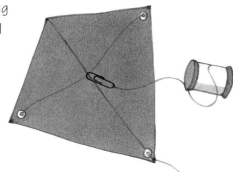

1. Fold your paper in half the long way.

2. Make a dot near the open edge of the paper, about one-third of the way down from the top. With a ruler, draw lines from the dot to the folded corners of the paper. Cut on these lines.

3. Unfold your paper. It should be shaped like a diamond. Punch holes inside the left, right, and bottom corners of the diamond. Stick paper reinforcements over the holes.

4. Cut a piece of string about 40 centimetres long. This will be the bridle of your kite. Put the ends of the string through the holes in the left and right corners of the diamond. Tie a big knot in each end.

5. Cut another piece of string about 51 centimetres long. This will be your kite's tail. Tie the string to the bottom corner of your kite.

6. Cut the paper handkerchief into four equal strips. Gently tie the strips onto the tail string. Don't pull too hard, or the paper will tear! Leave about eight centimetres between each bow.

7. Attach a paper clip to the bridle. Then tie a spool of string to the paper clip.

8. If you like, decorate your kite with markers or crayons.

Poems That Shine

Stars

Bright stars, light stars,
Shining-in-the-night stars,
Little twinkly, winkly stars,
Deep in the sky!

Yellow stars, red stars,
Shine-when-I'm-in-bed stars,
Oh how many blinky stars,
Far, far away!

—Rhoda W. Bacmeister

Firefly

A little light is going by,
Is going up to see the sky,
A little light with wings.

I never could have thought of it,
To have a little bug all lit,
And made to go on wings.

—Elizabeth Madox Roberts

27

The Bridge in the Sky

Long ago, people thought that rainbows were magic. Some people believed that a rainbow was a bridge for the gods to use when they wanted to come down to Earth. Other people believed that if you could find the end of a rainbow—where it touched the ground—you would find a pot of gold there.

Today, we know that rainbows are not magic. They are made by sunlight shining through raindrops. To see a rainbow, you must have the sun behind you and rain falling in front of you.

Sunlight looks white, but it really contains many colours. When sunlight enters a raindrop, it separates into violet, blue, green, yellow, orange, and red. We see these colours in the rainbow. Often, the colours blend, so we see only four or five of them.

A rainbow appears in the sky when many rays of sunlight separate into their colours and reflect off many raindrops. If the rain is heavy, the ends of the rainbow may appear to touch the ground.

It's a Fact
Turn on a hose. Adjust the water to a light spray. Stand with your back to the sun. You'll see a rainbow shining in the spray.

29

Up in the Air

Words and Music by Rebecca Rauff

We go up, up, up in the air, Sail-ing a - long, sing-ing a

song. We float high, low, fast or slow, Soar-ing a - long in the

air! Look down now! What do you see? I see a car! I see a

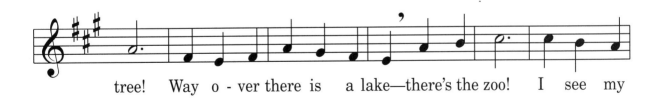

tree! Way o - ver there is a lake—there's the zoo! I see my

house! Do you see yours, too? It's so fun here up in the air,

Sail-ing a-long, sing-ing a song. We float high, low,

fast or slow, Soar-ing a-long in the air!

Clouds

White sheep, white sheep,
On a blue hill,
When the wind stops
You all stand still.

When the wind blows
You walk away slow.
White sheep, white sheep,
Where do you go?

—Christina Rossetti

★ Answer Key ★

For "The Creatures of Zorp," pages 14-15

Gliders have two legs. Stompers have four legs. Wigglers have six legs, and Hoppers have eight legs.

For "The Flight to Los Angeles," page 22

The pilot's last name is Navarro. The copilot's last name is Brooks. The flight engineer's last name is Lee.

Acknowledgements

The publishers of *Wonderful World of English* gratefully acknowledge the following publishers and authors for permission to reprint copyrighted text, and the following artists, photographers, and institutions for illustrations in this volume. All illustrations are the exclusive property of the publishers of *Wonderful World of English* unless names are marked with an asterisk (*).

1: Robert Byrd

2-3: Roberta Polfus
"Why the Sky is Blue" by John Ciardi. Copyright © 1974 by John Ciardi. Used with permission.

5-7: David Wenzel

8-9: Lucinda McQueen
"Moon-Come-Out" from *Over the Garden Wall* by Eleanor Farjeon. Copyright © 1933; renewed 1961 by Eleanor Farjeon. Reprinted by permission of HarperCollins Publishers./Recorded by permission of HarperCollins Publishers.

10-13: Robert Baxter

14-15: Diane Paterson

16-17: John Francis

18-21: Gwen Connelly

22: Ronald LeHew

23-24: Lydia Halverson

25: Len Ebert, Eileen Mueller Neill

26-27: Pam Johnson
"Stars" from *Stories to Begin On* by Rhoda Bacmeister. Copyright © 1940 by E. P. Dutton; renewed 1968 by Rhoda W. Bacmeister. Used by permission of Dutton Children's Books, a division of Penguin Books USA, Inc.
"Firefly" from *Under the Tree* by Elizabeth Madox Roberts. Copyright © 1922 by B. W. Huebsch Inc.; renewed 1950 by Ivor S. Roberts. Copyright © 1930 by Viking Penguin, Inc.; renewed 1958 by Ivor S. Roberts. Used by permission of Viking Penguin, a division of Penguin Books USA, Inc.

28-29: Eileen Mueller Neill

31: James Conahan

32: Gwen Connelly

Cover: Robert Byrd